Violoncello

LULL-A-BEAR
from *Ursa* (1990)

Robert Xavier Rodríguez

LULL-A-BEAR
from *Ursa* (1990)

Robert Xavier Rodríguez

Largo tranquillo
♩ = 54

ROBERT XAVIER RODRÍGUEZ

LULL-A-BEAR

FOR VIOLONCELLO AND PIANO

G. SCHIRMER, Inc.

DISTRIBUTED BY

HAL•LEONARD®

molto rall.   a tempo

pizz.,
molto vib.

ROBERT XAVIER RODRÍGUEZ

LULL-A-BEAR

FOR VIOLONCELLO AND PIANO

Composer's Note

Lull-A-Bear for cello and piano (1994) is a transcription which I made for Carlos Prieto of the third movement of my *Ursa: Four Seasons for Contrabass and Orchestra* (1990), commissioned by the National Endowment for the Arts for Gary Karr. As the title indicates, *Ursa* (Latin for "bear"), is programmatic. Like Vivaldi's famous violin concertos, my *Four Seasons* are based on texts, in this case fragments from four children's poems by Mary Medrick about a newborn bear and the discoveries and adventures of his first four seasons. *Lull-A-Bear* depicts a winter's hibernation, hence its subtitle, "Bear-ceuse," after the French *berceuse*, or cradle song. Carlos Prieto has recorded the work with Edison Quintano, piano (Urtext, JBCC014).

Duration ca. 2 minutes

ED 4308
First Printing October 2007

ISBN-13: 978-1-4234-1955-6
ISBN-10: 1-4234-1955-3

G. SCHIRMER, Inc.

DISTRIBUTED BY

HAL•LEONARD®
CORPORATION
7777 W. BLUEMOUND RD. P.O. BOX 13819 MILWAUKEE, WI 53213

G. SCHIRMER, Inc.

ISBN-13: 978-1-4234-1955-6
ISBN-10: 1-4234-1955-3

U.S. $12.95
ISBN-13: 978-1-4234-1955-6

Distributed By
HAL LEONARD

50486383

DISTRIBUTED BY
HAL•LEONARD®

51295

molto rall.   a tempo